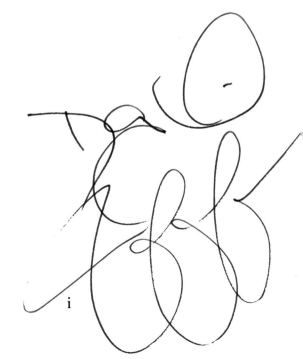

i

FROM "HEAR" TO FOREVER

FROM "HEAR" TO FOREVER

DANNY JEFFERSON
WITH RAYMOND REID

Alabaster Book Publishing
North Carolina

Published by Alabaster Book Publishing
P.O. Box 401
Kernersville, North Carolina 27285
www.PublisherAlabaster.biz

Book design by
David Shaffer

Cover art work by
Raymond Reid

First Edition

ISBN : 9780991266012

Library of Congress Control Number
2013958419

ACKNOWLEDGEMENTS

Obviously I could not start any acknowledgements without thanking our God who gave us life in the beginning. I was also blessed with two great parents who lead me regardless of which direction I was prone to go. Thank you Shirley Webb Jefferson and James Douglas Jefferson! I love you both!!!

This book is about life and how I was able to handle situations that affect numerous people every day. I wanted to possibly offer inspiration to others. Life is not easy and sometimes it can be cruel. We make it difficult ourselves and often it is difficult for no apparent reason. Humbled is the least I could say when I was approached about sharing experiences with others. I never would expect anyone to take the time to read a book about me, but I am convinced this book represents all of us who have had misfortunes in life. How we deal with those misfortunes is what will stamp our lives in the minds of those attending our own funeral.

I want to be remembered as someone who gave back more than was ever given to me. Giving isn't always about money. Sharing is contagious, and that is the main reason I agreed with Raymond in his writing this book.

Many people have helped me in my life. Mom, Dad, my sister Cindy, and many other family members were painting memories. My uncles, Ronnie and Kenneth Webb whose laughter inspired me to want to be funny, and they continue to light up my life today. Laughter was prevalent at every family function. Jokes were told, and I remembered them. Some weren't meant for my ears and were never repeated. (At least not that my Mom knew).

Childhood friends that I still have today include Ed and Lee Moser. We played and there was generally no fear. I continue to share friends with many classmates from Hillcrest Elementary, Turrentine Junior High, and Williams High School. We were young, foolish, and happy to paraphrase a line from an old "Beach Music" song. Regardless of what memories we have from any time in our lives, those memories shaped us into who we are today.

In the funeral profession I must thank

Wade Lowe(God rest his soul), Jim Lowe, Al Lineberry, Jr., and especially Al Lineberry, Sr. (and may God rest his soul as well). These men truly made an impact in my life and career. Little things too numerous to mention, and today may seem frivolous, have guided me in so many families lives.

Jack Pierce gave me a new lease on life at a crucial time in my life. He didn't know anything about my personal situation at the time, but wanted to partner with me for who he knew me to be in the funeral profession. To his entire family, Martha, Pam(God rest her soul), and Rick, my sincerest "Thanks". The Pierce family truly gave me an opportunity for a new lease on life.

My staff has allowed me time to confer with Raymond about this book. Randy McLean, a longtime funeral director in the community, has been the "piece that completed the puzzle". Randy is my friend. Debbie Mobley, Phil Bauguess, and all the staff of Pierce-Jefferson Funeral Service current and past I want to thank them all.

The spiritual guidance I have truly needed these last few years has been provided by my pastor and friend, Pete Kunkle. He and his wife Kathy have been an inspiration and cheerleaders along my journey. Thank you Pete and Kathy.

I would also like to thank Paul Dechant, who happens to be Father Paul to hundreds of his parishoners in the Catholic community. His friendship and wisdom will lead me through the rest of my life. Thank you, Paul.

Life friends are too numerous to mention but Dick Harlow is my brother in life. He has never wavered regardless of my circumstances. Bob Reed believed in me when no one else would give me a chance. Fagg Nowlan has offered so much in so many ways, and he never knew how much he was helping me. He just did it because that is who he is. Woody Garner was there when I truly had to have support. He also did not know how much he was helping me. Bob Prescott and Doug Marion who have listened when I wasn't trying to be funny. Thank you to all of you! My golfing buddies Spencer Smith, Alan Bennett, Craig "Smitty" Smith, and many more listened to my jokes and laughed. Thank you all!

My family, my son Jonathan Lee Jefferson and daughter Nikki Jefferson Kohut, continue to motivate me. My grandchildren Jack Kohut, Ramsey Jefferson, and Noah Kohut are a light that won't burn out.

Rosette Jefferson, my wife, is the greatest lady on the planet. She is an Angel and anyone that knows her will say the same. Thank you Rosette for being there for me, not judging me, and offering yourself to me when I was the only thing you could have. I know I would not be who I am if it were not for your compassion, understanding, and perseverance.

Again, I hope this book is an inspiration for anyone reading the stories. Read between the lines, guess what I was thinking, judge from the context of the situation, and love all those around you all the time.

For anyone who thought I was forgetting you by not including a name, I am truly sorry. Read from this list and I hope yours in on the list, LOL. Thank you Bo Fulton, Pete Howard, Steve Blackwell, Neal Stockton, Curtis Swisher, Charlie Vitow, Dawn Morgan, Randy Whicker, Mike Sasser, Clarence Lambe, Mike Lewis, Roger Stockton, Ron Saul, Steve Hutchins, Bill Apple, Keith Hill, Scott Henderson, Sam Jones, and an always insightful David Fitzpatrick. The spouses of all previously mentioned have been so supportive to me and I will forever be grateful.

TRIBUTE

Danny Jefferson...one word comes to mind immediately: heart.

When I first became acquainted with Danny, my impression was that he was a very outgoing, likeable and sincere individual. I was not wrong. But as I have gotten to know Danny much better, I had only begun to peel the layers off the outside of the onion. The best was yet to come.

By the nature of his chosen profession, it may not be too surprising that Danny sincerely cares for people, no matter what their station in life. Compassion is a prerequisite to success in the mortuary services business (ok, the <u>funeral home</u> business...now, I've said it!). But the intensity of his compassion far exceeds the requisite degree thereof for success. He feels it, he means it, and he extends it to so many people.

But the onion was not fully peeled after I merely got to know Danny a little better. As I served with him on numerous civic boards, and with him on several civic projects, I next thought that Danny was just a little too "gung ho" for his britches. But as our relationship continued to develop, I learned that Danny's "gung ho" was merely enthusiasm, unique creativity, and his zest for life, itself.

Having been on an extended vacation with Danny and his beautiful, extraordinary wife, Rosette, though, I learned that Danny's enthusiasm for life was not merely confined to his profession, or to his generous civic involvement. The man truly plays as hard as he works and serves. Frankly, the level of his enthusiasm while on vacation is equally intense…well, let me go ahead and say it… annoying! But it's more than likely that I am jealous of how hard he plays, and of how much fun he has while being involved in leisure activities.

I hear he's the same on golf trips. Although I do not personally engage in such a frivolous sport, those who do golf with him deserve, and receive, my most sincere sympathy!

All seriousness aside, Danny Jefferson is absolutely one of the finest, most dedicated citizens I have ever had the honor of knowing. He is a team player, in the final analysis. He always figures out how to get the job done, and somehow, how to get others to fall in behind him (or rather, with him).

Danny is unique, but he is a very good

and loyal friend.

Appreciatively submitted,
Bill Apple
Attorney at Law

TRIBUTE

Over the last eight years it has been great to get to know Danny on a professional and personal basis. We have developed what I feel is a close friendship where we can confide with each other whether it be on personal or business matters.

Danny is very easy to get to know as he so outgoing and has never met a stranger. He has a great personality that includes all attributes that you want to see in an individual. He is courteous, empathetic, trustworthy, honest, caring, thoughtful, witty, intelligent, professional and is faithful to his family and to his church.

I congratulate Danny on the success of his business since he came to Kernersville. He has jumped right in to the Kernersville Community giving many hours of his time to many community organizations and has supported this community financially.

Our community has been blessed by Danny.

Danny is a friend and will always be a friend!

Bob Reed
Senior Vice President, Fidelity Bank

TRIBUTE

Danny and I worked together years ago when he was doing standup. I believe it was at a one-nighter in Salisbury, NC. I got MARRIED in Salisbury years ago. Got DIVORCED in Concord, but hope to NEVER be buried or cremated in Kernersville.

Lance Montalto
Professional Standup Comedian

TRIBUTE

Acquaintance, friend of a friend, husband of an employee, employee, motivational speaker, professional manager, top producer, manager, life coach, entrepreneur, and my best friend! These are all descriptors I would use to describe my thirty-year relationship with Danny Jefferson.

I have witnessed Danny's evolution from an employee in a funeral home to the owner of one of the Southeast's best small businesses. Many people go to their job each day and very few are fortunate enough that their life's work is actually their vocation. Danny is just that kind of person. As the owner of Pierce Jefferson funeral home Danny has immersed himself in the local community and has served the needs of that community unlike any others.

This book, "From 'Hear' To Forever," takes you on a journey from modest beginnings in a mill town in North Carolina where a hearing impairment was not recognized initially to the man you will grow to respect and love as the complete professional. Some chapters will have you in tears and others will create broad smiles as you read, "From 'Hear' To Forever."

I have had two occasions in my life where very close relatives have passed away. In both cases my first instinct was to reach out to Danny for his help and support. With his help and counsel these very difficult times became more bearable. I know that as hundreds of families a year have relied on Danny for the same help and they have come away from the experience with the same feelings of comfort.

Dick Harlow
General Manager
Dick Broadcasting Company, Inc.

PROLOGUE

Raymond Reid

There's none so deaf as those that will not hear…
None so blind as those that will not see.

-Matthew Henry

If he's heard it once, he's heard it a thousand times: "Danny, you should write a book." No wonder. Words alone, though, cannot capture the essence, the aura… the countenance of Danny Jefferson.

His journey through life has seen its share of foggy nights, with failures here and there. Danny, though, sees failures as nothing less than opportunities. In the worst of times he always had a vision...a commitment to all things positive in his personal and professional life. Danny would bend, but he would never break. He overcame the adversity of being born legally deaf and all the stigmas associated with his handicap, like being laughed at and bullied. In spite of his deafness, he made very good grades. He made it all the way to the fourth grade before his teacher noticed that he couldn't hear. He was fitted for a hearing aid at Duke, which was awkward and bulky and, unbeknownst to his parents, he stopped wearing after a few months. At Duke a female staffer asked his dad how he planned to pay for the hearing aid, to which Mr. Jefferson replied, "I plan to pay cash." "Great, sir, then take your son to the front of the line."

Little Danny didn't understand. Even as a ten-year-old, he didn't think it was right to be treated better than anybody else. It left an indelible impression on him. To this day

Danny treats everyone exactly the same, regardless of their status in life. Millionaires and paupers are equal in his eyes. And if his employees don't follow his lead, they'll soon be looking for another job.

Danny himself was brought up poor in Burlington, N.C. where both of his parents were shift workers in textile mills. Only recently did he find out how much his hearing aid cost and how his dad paid for it. The cost was $675 and his dad paid for it with a year's worth of vacation money he had saved.

The Jefferson's had three children, Cindy, Danny and Terry. His sister Cindy was just eleven months and twenty-four days older. His little sister Terry was four years younger. Dinner at the Jeffersons often consisted of nothing but pinto beans and cornbread. But they always had enough to eat, thanks to Mrs. Jefferson. She hid money all over the place to keep Mr. Jefferson from "drinking it up" on beer and whiskey. After dinner they watched TV until bedtime.

Many years ago, though, Mr. Jefferson turned his life completely around. Today he and Mrs. Jefferson own their lovely home.

It's right beside Deep Creek Baptist Church in Burlington, where Mr. Jefferson has been a deacon for over forty-five years.

The little house in Burlington had only two bedrooms, one for Danny's parents and the other for his sisters. Danny slept in the hall. When everyone was asleep he would sneak into the den and turn the TV back on. The den was furnished with outdoor lawn furniture - aluminum with plastic mesh backs and seats. He would lie on his stomach and watch TV by peering through an opening in the mesh. Danny couldn't hear it thunder, much less *The Tonight Show*. So the sound was turned completely down. It was during those lonely, silent nights that he became an expert lip reader. And still is today.

How could one man overcome deafness to become a caring and compassionate funeral director and funeral home owner, civic leader, motivational speaker *and* a professional standup comedian? Well, you just have to know Danny Jefferson. And you're getting ready to...

WE COME INTO THIS WORLD
WITH NOTHING

*"Even Helen Keller, who was blind and deaf,
could see God."*

-Ray Comfort

They say when your death is imminent your entire life passes before your eyes. On September 14, 2004, my life was passing before my eyes, too. But I was dying a different kind of death. I was dying of humiliation. I had reached the bottom of the barrel that rainy and dreary night as I arrived at the Food Lion parking lot.

I chose the one several miles from home on the western side of Greensboro, North Carolina, so no one would recognize me. Because I wasn't there to buy groceries, I was there to cash in my loose change at the Coin Star machine. *"Pride goeth before the fall,"* says Proverbs 16:18. And I had become so proud that I was ashamed for anybody to see how broke I was. There I was at age 48. No wife. No money. No job. People have blown their brains out for less. But I never considered suicide. Never. But I had seen it first hand.

When I was sixteen years old and working part time for Lowe (rhymes with how) Funeral Home in Burlington, North Carolina, I was sent to a garage apartment in nearby Elon. A man had shot his wife in her left breast with a shotgun. (The murder had occurred the day before.) You could tell he had shot her point blank, probably from no more than a foot or two away. She was soaked in blood, which had splattered all over the place. Then he put the gun against the side of his head. You couldn't tell which side because his head was completely blown off. I was sent there to clean up the mess, because back then (in the early seventies) it was the funeral home's responsibility to take on the dirty work of cleaning up crime scenes. I found out later that the couple had a little five-year-old girl. It was her footprints that I saw that day. As I'm going up the steps to this little garage apartment I could see bloody little footprints coming down the steps. The blast was so powerful that blood had blown at least two feet through the crack at the bottom of the door. That little girl stood there and watched her dad kill her mother and then blow his own head off; then had to walk through his blood and brains to get out the door. She's a middle-age woman now and I often wonder what happened to her.

Life is a gift from God…and people don't understand that we're on this earth for such a short period of time. If you really truly put your mind to it - in the grand scheme of things - the Civil War was only yesterday. But too often, people lose their perspective and get caught up in the drama of the day; and can't go on.

Over the years I've embalmed many suicide victims who chose a permanent solution to a temporary problem. Suicide is a selfish act that destroys entire families. Choosing when we die is God's decision, not ours. And unless God took me that night, I would live to see another day. When I got back to my car I prayed to God to forgive me for many things, especially my pride and vanity. God had helped me overcome all the trials and tribulations that go with the territory when you're born legally deaf. Against all odds I had become a successful mortuary scientist/funeral professional, a sought after speaker, and a widely respected community and civic leader, with the honors and awards to prove it. I had even become a prominent stand up comedian. (Quite a feat when people used to laugh *at* me...not *with* me.)

Evidently, though, I believed I had gone it alone. I had taken all the credit, and not given God any. I, in my own mind, was invincible. No more. I closed my eyes and told God that if He got me through this mess I would be humble, gracious and thankful; and I would give back...*forever.* But the only thing I gave back that night was five percent to the Coin Star machine, which netted me \$142.38. It was every cent I had to my name. It wouldn't get me far, but at least I wouldn't starve (for a while.) I did have a feeling, though, that the worst was yet to come. I was waiting for the other shoe to fall.

And I wouldn't have to wait long...

HUMBLE BEGINNINGS ON WILDWOOD LANE

I stayed at a motel a few years ago and told the front desk person what time I needed to get up the next morning. I told him I couldn't hear so he would have to figure out a way to wake me up. So what did he do? He stuck a note under my door. Funny things like that have followed me around all my life. I consider myself lucky, though. Always have. When I was a kid there were five of us living in the little two- bedroom house at 218 Wildwood Lane in Burlington, North Carolina. My sisters, Cindy and

Terry shared a bedroom. My parents, James and Shirley slept in the other one. I camped out in the hall. We moved to Burlington in 1959 from another little house in Roxboro, North Carolina…the house in which my sister Cindy and I were born. Terry was born in Burlington in an actual hospital.

Back then, Burlington was nothing but a textile town. Those were the heydays for textile giants like Burlington Industries, Cone Mills and Glen Raven Mills, where my dad was a shift worker. Dad later went to work for the Cone Mills Haw River plant in the cutting department, which made the grooves in corduroy fabrics. Mom worked at home mending hosiery for a company called Hole-N-None. When we were older, she went to work at Annedeen Hosiery, where she worked in the pairing department. This was decades before NAFTA came along and textile jobs went away by the thousands to China and Mexico. Today Burlington, because of its location halfway between the Triad and the Triangle, is a shopping Mecca with outlet malls all over the place. It also has more restaurants per capita than any city in the United States.

Burlington was a town of "haves" and "have nots." And the Jefferson family certainly fit into the latter category. We didn't exactly live on the wrong side of the tracks, but calling our neighborhood modest would be an understatement. But we were just a few blocks away from the more affluent neighborhoods.

A guy by the name of Ed Moser lived in one of those neighborhoods. We were about the same age and became good friends. He never looked down his nose at me. And his parents always welcomed me into their home. Ed and I have become lifelong friends, and I talk with him often.

The crime rate back then was almost zero. I'm not sure we even locked our doors. One thing was for sure, though, Cindy and I walked several blocks to Hillcrest Elementary School every day without worry. Things like Amber Alerts were unheard of in those days.

Although I couldn't hear, I managed to make good grades. I had learned to read lips by sneaking into the living room and turning on the TV after everyone had gone to bed. I'm sure my parents sensed something wasn't quite right with me, but they let it slide. Dad especially got irritated at me and yelled a lot when my back was turned to him. He took a belt to me more than once, especially when he was drinking, which was most of the time. Normal stuff back then, though. He was not abusive to my sisters or me for sure; nor to my mom. She simply wouldn't have put up with it.

When I was five or six, I remember dad being particularly irritated. He stormed into the house late one afternoon and yelled, "Danny, get out here fast. Help me get these damn nails out of the driveway." He explained to me that the labor union at Glen Raven had gone on strike. I didn't understand what a picket line was, but he said he had "crossed it." "I can't afford to miss any work, Danny," he said. "I've got a family to feed. Those union bastards are getting back at me. Guess they didn't think I'd see these nails and I'd end up with four flat tires."

I remember being scared and wondering what else they might do. From then on, we made sure all the doors were locked. Overall, though, I considered my childhood to be relatively normal. We always had clean clothes to wear and enough food on the table, even if it was just pinto beans and cornbread. And we had to eat everything on our plates. That was a strict order. There was always enough money to pay for essentials, thanks to my mother. She hid what little money she made from Hole-N-None all over the place. If she hadn't, dad would have spent it on booze. Our biggest treat when we were little was going to Biff Burger for dinner on payday. I'm not sure why we went to Biff Burger instead of McDonald's, I guess because it was cheaper. Strict rules there, too. If I ordered two burgers and an order of fries I'd better eat every crumb.

They say you can fool some of the people some of the time, but not all of the people all of the time. I got all the way to the fourth grade with my deafness going practically undetected. But I couldn't fool my fourth grade teacher. She called my mother and set up a meeting with her and me. "Mrs. Jefferson," she said. "Danny has a problem paying attention. His grades are okay, but I have to make him sit at the front of the class. Otherwise, he just doesn't respond when I call his name…or ask him a question. I believe he needs to see a doctor. I think he has a serious hearing problem." Mother didn't act a bit surprised. I'm sure she knew it all along. The next day mother took me to see Dr. Gaddy in Burlington for tests.

"Mrs. Jefferson," said Dr. Gaddy, "This boy can barely hear a lick. He needs a hearing aid and I'm going to refer you to the audiology center down at Duke Hospital." The appointment was set for the next week. Mom, Dad and I took the forty-five minute trip and got there thirty minutes early. Punctuality is how they operated. When you're used to punching a clock and getting paid by the hour, you always arrive early.

We finally found the audiology center and Dad signed us in. When they asked Dad how he was going to pay, he said, "Cash, of course." The other people must have been on welfare or were setting up payments, because the nurse said, "Okay, you all can go to the front of the line." I remember not understanding. I didn't think it was fair for us to go to the front of the line. We were escorted into the doctor's office a few minutes later and I was given a battery of tests, and fitted for a hearing aid. This was in 1966 and hearing aid technology was not very advanced. What I was fitted with was called a "body" hearing aid. I think it was a transistor hearing aid and made by Zenith. The earplugs were attached to a little amplifier about the size of a pack of cigarettes that contained batteries. You put in the earplugs, and ran the cord under your shirt, and hooked the little amplifier onto your belt. It was very awkward and uncomfortable and really didn't work very well. I only recently found out that the cash dad paid, $695, was vacation money he had saved. A lot of money, considering he was only making $1.25 an hour.

By the time I was in the fifth grade, I got tired of wearing the hearing aid. I was embarrassed by it. And it certainly looked stupid when I was trying to play basketball. I was pretty good at basketball, too. So good, as a matter of fact, that I made the team at Turrentine Junior High School. It was at about that time, when I was fourteen, that dad became a born again

Christian. He immediately quit smoking. And he immediately quit drinking. Cold turkey! He went from one extreme to the other: From never going to church to going every time the doors opened, including twice on Sunday plus every Wednesday night. Problem was my basketball games were on Wednesday night and I had to go to church when my dad went. My excuse for the first game that I missed was that my grandmother died. Grandmothers can't die but so many times, so I had to quit the team.

But I did play baseball for one year. I even won Most Valuable Player for a city league team. None other than Hall of Famer Enos Slaughter presented me my trophy. Ironically, the team I played for was sponsored by the same labor union that put the nails in our driveway!

I didn't play anymore after that, though. It just wasn't worth the hassle because of having to go to church all the time.

FROM PUMPING GAS TO
BOARDING SOCKS

When I was in high school at Burlington Williams I got a job at a local service station. Back then there were real service stations, where you not only pumped gas, you checked the oil, tire pressure and even cleaned the windshield. The owner had a lot of confidence in me and would often leave to run errands and leave me there to run the place. But I had a tough time because of my hearing problem. And customers would get aggravated with me when I couldn't understand how much gas they wanted. So

I longed for a job where I wouldn't have to interact with people. My mother was finally able to land me a job on the second shift at Annedeen Hosiery, where she had been moved to the pairing department. I got there right after school and worked from three until eleven.

My job was boarding socks (the process of putting creases in the socks), thirty-six at a time, pulling them from boxes that each contained a hundred dozen pairs. I was on "piece work" but no matter how many socks I was able to board during my shift, the money always seemed to equal out. About all I could average were a box and a half per shift. That added up to a little over minimum wage. It was a meticulous job that required standing up for the entire eight-hour shift. The plant was not air-conditioned and the heat was brutal. Some of the workers in there were "lifers," who had been doing this monotonous job for twenty or thirty years.

One guy, named Henry Frye, had been doing this all his adult life. He was somewhere in his fifties. You could set your watch by him. He would get in a little before three and punch the time clock. You weren't allowed to punch in earlier than ten minutes before your shift started. The shift started at three, and that's when your pay started. If you punched in after three, you were "docked," two minutes for every one - minute you were late. But Henry was never late. He was there on time every day, with his lunch box and drink in hand. When the bell rang at three, he would get up onto the boarding machine, and not a minute before. He would stop religiously for his break, and he would stop religiously for his meal. He would sit there and eat while staring into space, rarely talking with anyone. Ten minutes later he was back on the machine. When the bell rang at eleven o'clock he packed up and went home.

That was the life of a mill worker in the early 1970s. And it would be the only life that Henry Frye and thousands of textile workers in Burlington, including my parents, would ever know. I knew, though, that I was not going to follow in my parents' footsteps and spend my life toiling in a textile mill. I just hoped something would come along that would be more fulfilling for me. On May 1, 1972 it did. That was the day I went to work at Lowe Funeral Home in Burlington.

As menial as it was (washing family cars and hearses, and erecting gravesite tents) it was a good job. And the catalyst for what would become my life's work.

NIGHTMARE ON HIGHWAY 87

I was very proud of my job at Lowe. And as it turned out I did more than just wash the funeral home's vehicles and erect graveside tents. I often went with funeral directors to pick up bodies at nursing homes and hospital morgues. Hearses are always used for this task. Anytime you see a hearse alone on the highway it's almost always on its way to pick up a body, or is returning to the funeral home with one. Otherwise, you only see hearses in slow moving funeral processions. You will never see hearses exceeding the speed limit. Well…almost never. Enter Jim Lowe, the son of the funeral home's owner, Wade Lowe.

Jim loved to drive fast. He loved fast cars and pushed them to the limit. As a professional funeral director, though, he reserved his pedal to the metal mentality for cars…not hearses; but not always.

On a rainy night in 1973 Jim asked me to ride with him to pick up a body at a nursing home down in Lee County near Sanford. We had just finished up an embalming when the call came in around midnight. It had been a long day and we were both very tired. The hearse we were in that night was a light blue 1963 Cadillac; the one with the big fins on the back. For years it had been used as an ambulance back when funeral homes were in the EMS business. When there was an emergency people would call the telephone operator who then called local funeral homes. The funeral homes dispatched their ambulances whose drivers raced to see who could get to the scene first. If there was a dead body there, or the person died later in the hospital, the funeral home that arrived first usually got the embalming and funeral business. So speed was important, not only in getting to the accident site, but oftentimes rushing the victim to the hospital. But big, awkward Cadillacs, unlike today's EMS vehicles, were not safe to drive at high speeds. And there were plenty of wrecks to prove it.

On this particular night, Jim must have thought he was on an emergency call; and had forgotten that what used to be an ambulance was now a hearse. He was flying down dark, rainy and dreary Highway 87 and I was holding on for dear life. I was praying that this thing wouldn't run off the road and hit a tree. What a way to go, I thought. *Getting killed in a hearse!*

"Jim," I exclaimed. "What's the hurry? This lady's dead and she'll still be dead when we get there!"

"Sorry, Danny, I just remember back when this puppy had a siren and flashing red lights and I raced it to the scene...trying to get there before the other guys."

"Well," I said, "The County took over the ambulance business several months ago. That means you're driving a hearse now, Jim...not an ambulance. A HEARSE! I'm just seventeen and you're just twenty-six. We embalm people, Jim. I'm not ready for someone to embalm *me!*"

"Well," Jim said. "I'll slow down a little bit, at least until the rain lets up."

"I hope so. This trip's been way too exciting, and I didn't bring a change of underwear."

We finally arrived at the depressing little nursing home that was somewhere between Sanford and nowhere. I joked that it was not the end of the world, but we could see it from there. A rotund and disheveled nurse in her sixties met us at the door and said, "If you're the undertakers we've been expecting you. Please follow me." No small talk with her. No introductions. No "nothing." It was all business. She led us down a dimly lit (and smelly) hallway to the last door on the left, where a tiny woman was lying on her back on a small hospital bed.

"How long has she been dead?" Jim asked.

"Sometime this afternoon," the nurse replied. "We finally tracked down her daughter in Burlington tonight and that's when you were called."

"Okay, Danny," said Jim. "It's a long

drive back to Burlington. Let's get her out of here."

Back then we used two-man stretchers. That's all we had. One-man stretchers (that had wheels) to allow one person to load by themselves may have come along by then, but we didn't own one. So it would take both of us to carry her out to the hearse, although she probably didn't weigh over eighty pounds. We pulled away the sheet that was covering her body to reveal a gruesome sight: She only had one arm and one leg. How shocking and sad. I knew, though, that if I stayed in this business long enough I would see a lot worse than that. We hauled her out, loaded her into the back of the hearse, and were off to the races - literally. Lead foot Jim was at it again, flying up the road toward Burlington.

Highway 87 back then was two lanes all the way, and very hilly and curvy. The sun was just beginning to come up and we hadn't had a wink of sleep. For some reason Jim looked into the rearview mirror and screamed, "Lord! There's nothing back there Danny. Where in the hell did she go?" Then he starts slamming on the brakes and orders me to get out of the hearse and see what's going on. "Yes sir Jim," I said. So I jumped out. Problem was the hearse had not come to a complete stop. I was wearing slick bottom boots that provided no traction whatsoever. I immediately slipped and fell flat on my face. Bleeding, I crawled to the back of the hearse and opened the door. And to my horror the lady came tumbling out onto the highway, mattress and all. Evidently Jim's erratic driving had caused her to fall off the stretcher and onto the floor.

So there she was – a corpse with one arm and one leg - lying on the double yellow line in the middle of Highway 87. About that time I saw headlights coming over the hill about fifty yards behind us. And they weren't just any headlights. They belonged to an eighteen -wheeler. The driver started blowing his horn and gearing down. Jim jumped out of the hearse and yelled, "Oh, %#@*!"

Together, we scooped up the poor old lady, blankets, mattress and all, and had to literally throw her back into the hearse. We slammed the door and ran to the other side right as the eighteen-wheeler roared by. Then Jim made me get back there, put her back on the stretcher, and stay with her for the remainder of the trip to Burlington. There were no straps on the stretcher so I had to hold onto her. If I hadn't, she would have fallen off again...because Jim continued his crazy driving.

When we finally got back to town we decided to have breakfast before embalming the poor soul. As soon as we entered our favorite breakfast place, the Oak Grove Diner, a waitress asked me what in the world happened to my face? "Well," I quipped, "you should see the other guy."

After breakfast, and several cups of coffee, Jim looked me right in the eye and said, "Danny, you need to promise me something." "Uh...what would that be, Jim?"

"You need to promise me, on a stack of Bibles, that you will never tell my daddy what happened with that poor old lady."

It was a promise I didn't keep. About five years later I told Mr. Lowe the whole story of what happened that morning. Mr. Lowe, chuckling, said, "You know Danny...I remember that old lady. And wondered how in God's name she got those road burns on her face!"

THE SHOTGUN FUNERAL

The "Releasing of the Doves" ritual has long been a part of memorial ceremonies at graveside services. We had such a request in 1976 when I was working at Lowe. The funeral was conducted at a little Baptist church in Saxapahaw, a tiny mill town on the Haw River in a remote area of Alamance County. A recently harvested cornfield down in a valley surrounded the church and adjacent cemetery. It was a beautiful setting against a cloudless sky in early September.

After the funeral, which was very long

even by Baptist standards, six pallbearers carried the casket to the gravesite, which was about thirty yards from the church. There are two kinds of dove releases; one is a twelve - dove release in which a single dove is released, representing the soul of the deceased, followed by twelve doves. For this service, the family chose the three - dove release, which represents the "Trinity:" The Father, The Son and The Holy Ghost. A fourth dove, representing the soul of the deceased, is then released. Although they are called doves, they are actually homing pigeons. A member of the family opened a basket and released three doves, then the fourth. The doves then circled the gravesite three times and flew away.

It was a beautiful, final touch to a very emotional, but uplifting service. And it went off without a hitch. Almost. The doves had hardly disappeared over a hill above the cornfield when the unmistakable sound of shotgun blasts rang out. BOOM! BOOM! BOOM! BOOM! *It was the first day of dove season!*

MY CHARLIE ANGEL

When I was a senior in high school, Charlie Vitou, from the North Carolina Office on Disability, contacted me. He informed me that I qualified for State assistance because of my family's income level and, "For overcoming the severe handicap of being legally deaf to finish near the top of your class." The assistance included paying half of my college tuition at Gupton-Jones School of Mortuary Science and the use of a State owned hearing aid. It was one of the happiest days of my life. And I will forever be indebted to Charlie

Vitou. I admire him until this day. And he's always given back to the community. Even now he is president of the Exchange Club in Elon, North Carolina.

I couldn't wait to tell the folks at Lowe Funeral Home who had so graciously introduced me to the business. Albeit humble, it sure beat pumping gas at the service station and boarding socks at Annedeen Hosiery. I have fond memories of putting up tents and washing cars at Lowe. And I won't forget the first suit they bought me... a blue, casual suit. Something like Sonny Bono wore, except a lot darker. I started at the bottom, for sure. But in a year or so, I would be a licensed funeral director with a degree in mortuary science. Before enrolling, though, I was sent back to Duke to reassess my hearing.

The State would provide me with a new hearing aid, for which they would hold the title for five years (to keep me from selling it.) They would also pay half of my college tuition as long as I maintained above a "C" average. At Duke, Dr. Chris Brutomesso screened me. After giving me a battery of hearing tests she said, "Considering the extent of his hearing loss, I don't know how he even passed high school, much less got into the National Honor Society!"

I prayed and thanked God for giving me the strength to overcome my handicap. I thanked my parents and hugged them both. I'll never forget what they've done for me. They loved me and sacrificed for me.

For example, I was at a funeral one day in the dead of winter, wearing just the blue casual suit the folks at Lowe bought me. I thought I was going to freeze to death. I kept ducking behind the church to get out of the wind. I told my mother that I really needed an overcoat. Although she couldn't afford it, she bought me one the next week. Mother is a saint, if there ever was one.

Thank you, Mom. Thank you, Dad. And thank you again Charlie Vitou, for coming into my life!

MAY THE (AIR) FORCE BE WITH ME?

After graduating from high school I was secure knowing (thanks to Charlie Vitou) that half my tuition to Gupton-Jones School of Mortuary Science was covered. I was afraid, though, that I wouldn't be able to pay for the other half.

I found out the U.S. Air Force had a mortuary corps and the training would be free. I would be able to serve my country and get a government paid education at the same time. What a deal! So...I called the recruiters in Raleigh and told them I wanted to join the Air Force. They set up a time for me to come down there and get a physical examination. A few days later I received two bus tickets to Raleigh...round trip tickets, you might say. I didn't tell anyone at Lowe Funeral Home what I was up to. I just said I needed to take a day off for some personal business.

The bus trip was uneventful and we arrived at the recruitment office around 10:00 a.m. There were about thirty of us. After we signed in and had our identities verified, we were given gym shorts and T-shirts and told where to report. We were given a battery of tests including push- ups and running on a treadmill. Then came an EKG, a hernia test, urine test, and a close look into our eyes, ears and down our throats. So far, so good, I thought. But then it was time for the hearing test.

They put us in booths, four on one side and four on the other with an aisle in between. They closed the doors and started the test. The noise tests varied in volume; high, low and middle. Each of us had headphones and buttons to push and was instructed to push it every time we heard a buzz. Well, I just randomly started pushing the button. I'd wait a few seconds and start pushing it again. After about two minutes the sergeant who was administering the test came storming into my booth. He jerked back the headphones, got right in my ear and yelled, "Jefferson!" "Yes, sir," I replied. "Quit pushing the damn button unless you hear the buzzes." Then he stormed out and slammed the door. And I just kept pushing the button, hoping I'd get lucky.

That afternoon we were called together for further instructions, and retests if necessary. That's when I got yelled at again. "Jefferson," the sergeant blurted out, "Report back to the hearing test center immediately." He probably wondered how I even heard his screaming instructions. I didn't. I read his lips. So back to the hearing test center I went. And again I started randomly pushing the button. Same result. I had officially failed the hearing test, miserably. I was classified as 4-F and sent home.

I can always say, however, that I tried to serve my country in the U.S. Air Force. And I really thought I could fake it well enough to pass the hearing test. But it wasn't meant to be. Now I was back to plan one: Gupton-Jones - and no way to pay the other half of my tuition.

My life, though, was about to make another turn...at a nightclub in Greensboro. Everything would take care of itself after that, tuition and all – or so I thought.

BE YOUNG… BE FOOLISH

In the 1960s and 70s Bill Griffin was a nightclub owner and promoter who reached legendary status in Greensboro. His clubs included the Boondocks, Castaways and Bill Griffin's Underground - a club that often packed in hundreds of people - to dance to the era's most popular soul, beach and R&B entertainers: The groups included the Drifters, General Johnson and the Chairmen of the Board, the Embers, the Part-Time-Party-Time Band and Doug Clark and the Hot Nuts. It was a scene that I loved and a great way to relieve the occupational stress of the funeral business.

It was at one of Griffin's clubs, the Castaways, where I met Donna. She was from the Archdale, N.C. area. We loved the party scene and got caught up in the moment. Lyrics from "Fools Fall in Love," by the Drifters could have been written for Donna and me: *Fools fall in love in a hurry. Fools give their hearts much too soon. They're making plans for the future, when they should be back in school.* And school is exactly where I was headed.

Knowing that my calling was to be in the funeral business, my next stop would be Gupton-Jones, and off I went. Donna and I promised to stay in close touch. One thing led to another and our fate had been sealed. A wedding date was set for December 28, 1975. I planned my studies at the college so I would graduate in one year instead of two; four straight semesters with no time off, except for holidays.

There were no dormitories back then at Gupton-Jones so students had to make their own living arrangements. Three other guys and I lived at Atlanta's largest funeral home, H.M. Patterson & Sons, which had been established in 1882. We were at the Cascade location.

Patterson was very well known and highly regarded. On April 12, 1945, President Franklin D. Roosevelt died of a cerebral hemorrhage at his home in Warm Springs, Georgia. On the same day, Patterson "undertakers" were summoned there to prepare his body for the "funeral train" to Washington, D. C.

I loved college and did quite well. I was particularly fascinated by the history of embalming. I learned how embalming was done in ancient Egypt. The bodies were first washed in water from the Nile. Then the organs, except for the heart, were removed, washed and packed in natron, (a hydrous native sodium carbonate), and placed in clay jars. The heart was left intact, because it would be needed in the afterlife. The brain was removed with a long hook and pulled out through the nose. The body was then covered with natron. After forty days the body was again washed and covered with oils. Then, the dehydrated organs were wrapped in linen and returned to the body. Lastly, the body was covered once more with oils and wrapped in linen. The pyramids, actually, are nothing more than mausoleums, filled with mummies.

Modern day embalming, I learned, didn't become popular in the United States until the Civil War, when there was a need to preserve dead bodies for the return trip home. A surgeon, Thomas Holmes, is credited with developing a safe, nontoxic embalming fluid - four ounces of arsenic per gallon of water. Holmes accepted a commission as captain in the U.S. Medical Corps, and set up embalming tents after each Civil War battle.

At Gupton-Jones, there was a lot to learn besides embalming. There were intensive course studies in history, chemistry, English literature, business math, counseling and microbiology. Embalming, though, was the most challenging course of all. It was certainly the course that led to a high drop out rate at the college.

Better to embalm than to get embalmed, and one night I was almost the latter. At least I thought was going to be. I woke up one morning around two o'clock with horrible pains in my stomach and lower back. They say kidney stones are like having a baby. Thank God men can't have babies or there would be no babies. I screamed and woke up my buddies, Tom Bullard and Jim Davis who were sleeping down the hall at H. M. Patterson. "Get me to the hospital, guys," I yelled. "I think I'm dying." Tom and Jim came running in to my room, picked me up and hauled me out to the garage. Then they threw me into the back of a hearse and sped up the road toward Fulton County Hospital.

When the hearse came to a screeching halt in front of the emergency room, a security guy ran out and said, "You guys can't park that thing here. And this is not where you pick up bodies." "Hell," replied Tom, "we're not here to pick up a body, we're hear to deliver one!"

Well, as it turned out, it was not my time to go. I passed the stone several hours later. And it would not be my last bout with kidney stones. I've had six more (so far).

My next trip to the hospital, though, would be for an entirely different reason.

'TILL DEATH DO US PART

Donna and I got married during my Christmas break from school on December 28, 1975, as planned. I graduated six months later at the top of my class and went to work full time at Lowe Funeral Home in Burlington. Donna and I decided to live in Burlington and bought a house there for $24,000.

She was unhappy from the beginning, however, and longed to live back in Archdale. Her dad offered us some land there and we built a house, right beside of his. By then I had accepted a job at nearby Sechrest

Funeral Home in High Point. Donna also desperately wanted to get pregnant and we were having no luck at all. Fertility tests revealed no problems with Donna. Turns out that I was the one who had the problem. Tests revealed that I had vericocele veins along my spermatic chord, which greatly limited my sperm count. Surgery (at High Point Regional Hospital) was required to rectify this problem, and it worked.

Right around that time an event that happened in Guyana disturbed me greatly. Only the terrorist attack of 9-11 claimed more American lives. The Reverend Jim Jones had recently moved his cult, the Peoples Temple, from San Francisco to this remote jungle. The original roots of the cult go back to Indiana, Jones' home state. Seems that word had gotten to Washington, in particular, to California Congressman Leo Ryan, that people were being held in Guyana against their will. So Ryan and four of his associates went down to take a look. Jones realizing that government was closing in forced his followers into a mass suicide by drinking poisoned Kool Aid. Those who didn't participate were shot. All told,

909 brainwashed "worshippers" were dead. Ryan and his associates were ambushed at the nearby airstrip and shot to death.

When Ryan failed to return, the U.S. Air Force sent a helicopter in to see what happened. They counted 300 bodies and requested exactly that many wooden caskets, which were flown in by an Air Force C-130 transport plane. Bodies were stacked on top of one another. Removing the first 300 revealed 300 more, requiring 300 more caskets be flown in. Finally, 309 more bodies were revealed so that many more caskets were ordered. Each body had to be placed in an individual wooden casket. The bodies were rotting and falling apart. The stench was unbearable. Air Force members used cinnamon oil inside their dust masks to help block the smell. The bodies were flown back to a hangar in Baltimore for embalming. The stench was so bad on those flights that the crew had to wear oxygen masks. Three civilian morticians, at taxpayer expense, embalmed all 909 bodies.

As an embalmer myself, I can't imagine how difficult that task was. I've had to do some gruesome embalmings during my career, but never one involving numerous bodies that were decomposing. I've always had strong beliefs regarding good and evil. God is at work in the world, and so is the devil. In my opinion, people who don't believe this are fools. Jim Jones was the devil personified. He was as evil as Adolph Hitler.

When people commit suicide, I believe a demonic spirit has taken over. And when a person has Alzheimers, that person is no longer with us. He or she, in my opinion, has gone on to Heaven. What's left has been taken over by a negative spirit.

But I had more immediate things to be concerned about. Thanks to my surgery, Donna was soon pregnant.

SPINNING WHEEL
GOT TO GO ROUND

Our son, Jonathan, was born in 1979. Then things started going downhill. There was just so much pressure on Donna and me, financial and otherwise. Simply, we were young and immature. Way too young to be married, much less have children. Everything began to unravel, especially my relationship with her father. Simply, what I thought was gift money for half of my tuition wasn't a gift at all, according to him. He wanted his money back. He also wanted the money for the land next door to him, which I also thought was a gift. I felt pressured and completely smothered. Confused. In my heart of hearts, I knew I had to get out. So I walked away.

It was the hardest thing I ever had to do. But one thing was for sure, though. I would take care of my son, financially. I just could not continue living with his mother. Looking back, I know I made the right decision. But I made a huge mistake, too...I left without consulting with a lawyer. Like I said, HUGE MISTAKE. One thing was for sure, though. It didn't take Donna and her dad long to hire a lawyer. Simply, the law said that I walked out on my family. And I didn't have a leg to stand on. I did hire a lawyer, but it didn't help much. When my lawyer and their lawyer worked out the "deal," my child support was $380 a month. And I was only making $800 a month.

Donna remarried soon after our divorce was final. I was over a barrel. By then I was $3,500 behind in child support. The debt would be forgiven and future child support absolved under one condition: That I give Jonathan up for adoption. Period. The agreement was clear: If I contacted

Jonathan before he was eighteen years old, I would go to jail. Signing those papers was a horrible experience. But I had no choice. There was no way I could come up with money to get out of this mess.

Living without being able to communicate with my son would be hell on earth. Jon was my flesh and blood and my heart would never heal. They say that outliving a child is the worst thing that can happen to a parent. I agree. But the next worse thing is being banned from watching your child grow up… and being there for him. It was the price I had to pay. And it hurt me to the bottom of my soul. Simply, I felt cheated. Cheated out of eighteen years of things that fathers and sons do together. First day of school; T-ball; Little League; his first bout with puppy love; going to the movies and ball games. Watching Monday Night Football together; shooting pool…playing catch and badminton in the backyard. Putting my arm around him and comforting him when he is down and out. Not even being able to talk to him on the phone. Father's Day will be my saddest day of the year.

I will think about Jon every day. But

the law is the law. And I sure didn't want to go to jail. So I signed, left, and moved into a house in High Point with a friend of mine, Rocky Carter, a guy I knew at the Dale Carnegie Institute. After a couple of months I moved into an apartment, also in High Point, with one of Rocky's friends.

In December 1979 I left Sechrest and went to work for Hanes Lineberry Funeral Home in Greensboro.

It didn't take long for my life to hit another bump in the road.

"MINE EYES HAVE SEEN THE GLORY..."

A guy who worked at Hanes Lineberry, Tolbert Stroud, was not only a veteran embalmer and funeral professional, he also was a retired U.S. Army sergeant, with twenty years of service. His name may have been Tolbert, but everyone knew him as "Sarge." He was military in every sense of the word. Everything he did was by the book. He was regimented in everything he did. And he was none too friendly toward me. And those feelings would get worse before they got better.

Just a month after I was hired Mr.

Lineberry called me into his office and said, "Jefferson, I have a lot of confidence in you; so much confidence that I'm going to make you head embalmer. Now I won't mention any names, son, but this isn't going to sit well with certain individuals in this funeral home. Sarge in particular is going to be royally peeved. But don't come running to me if he gives you a hard time. You're a grown man, Jefferson. And you're going to have to handle it all by yourself."

"I don't know what to say Mr. Lineberry," I stammered. "I'm honored and flattered that you would put me ahead of the other guys. I'll handle Sarge…and you have my word that you will be proud of me. I won't let you down." "I know you won't Jefferson…I know you won't."

I left Mr. Lineberry's office on cloud nine. I was elated to have this kind of responsibility placed on my shoulders. But at the same time I was dreading the fallout. The resentment. The jealousy. I felt, though, that I deserved the head embalmer's position. I had the experience and the top-notch educational credentials needed to be an upper echelon mortuary scientist. But I knew deep down that I was going to have serious problems with Sarge. In his mind I was still wet behind the ears. And frankly, he didn't like me, even before I got the promotion. Everything I did rubbed him the wrong way. We almost came to blows one day at the funeral home's old Vanstory location.

We were downstairs with a guy I very much admired named Bill Newnam. Bill was a good man...a good father, who had six children - three of his own and three foster kids. He spent the night at the funeral home to make extra money for his family. He drove an old Plymouth Valiant with a rusted hole in the floorboard, which was covered by a piece of plywood. I'm not sure what stirred up the fracas that day, but Sarge and I almost came to blows. We would have if Bill hadn't stepped in between us. I weighed just 150 pounds at the time and Sarge was huge. I'm certain if Bill hadn't been there to break up the fight that Sarge would have killed me. There is no doubt in my mind. My relationship with Sarge continued to fester and fester. I was scared to death of him.

One day I was looking through the files of people who had pre-planned their funeral arrangements. I noticed a file labeled with the name Tolbert Stroud. I was not surprised that the regimented Sarge would plan every aspect of his life...and death. His form listed pallbearers and "honorary" pallbearers. Honorary pallbearers were supposed to include the staff of Hanes Lineberry. Sarge listed his honorary pallbearers as, "The staff of Hanes Lineberry, LESS JEFFERSON." His "wishes" went on to say that, "Jefferson could not be anywhere on the premises" during his funeral service. I decided right then to try and get along with Sarge as a fellow funeral director, but that's all. I would avoid being alone with him day or night at all costs. I was literally afraid for my life.

Then one night he showed up. I was hanging out late with Bill Newnam after completing the embalming of an elderly lady we had picked up at Moses Cone Hospital. "I need to talk with you Jefferson... alone," Sarge said. "Can you please come with me?" He was blocking the door and I couldn't escape. So I turned to Newnam and said, "Bill, I'm going with him. And if I'm not back in fifteen minutes, call the police." I walked up the steps ahead of Sarge and considered running away. Everything was racing through my mind. Was he going to beat me up? Was he going to kill me? I made a commitment to myself right then that I would hold my own. I would not let him bully me around. My adrenaline had kicked up a notch. I was ready for anything.

When we reached the top of the stairs I turned right and headed to one of the front parlors. There was a door leading out to a porch and large windows on both sides. So I knew that I could possibly escape unless, of course, he had a gun. I turned around as we entered the room and looked Sarge right in the eye. There were tears in his eyes. "Jefferson," he said. "I've wronged you. I've been hurtful to you. I have disappointed my family and everyone here at the funeral home. I don't know what's been wrong with me. All I can say Jefferson is, I'm sorry. I'm very, very sorry. I want to call a truce…and I want to call it tonight." By then I, too, was fighting back tears. We shook hands and then embraced. Sarge began sobbing… about a month later he went down to the

V.A. hospital in Salisbury for a routine check up. It didn't turn out to be routine at all. Sarge was diagnosed with liver cancer.

They sent him home and gave him three months to live. When he arrived from the hospital I was the first person there to greet him. We went inside, hugged each other and had a good cry. A few weeks later his condition had greatly deteriorated. There was no hospice back then so he was at home. He called me and said he needed to talk. I went to his house and his wife, Ramona, led me down the hall to a dimly lit bedroom. I sat down on a small stool beside his bed. He looked gaunt and jaundiced and had lost a ton of weight. He took my hand and said, "Jefferson, I need to change my funeral plans. And I want you to embalm me. And I want you to dress me. Nobody is to mess with my body but you."

He died three weeks later at two o'clock in the morning. Ramona called me and said, "Danny...the battle is over." "Hang in there, dear," I said. "We'll be there in a few minutes." At the time I was rooming with my lifelong friend, Steve Blackwell. So I woke him up and told him about Sarge.

Steve and I drove to the funeral home, picked up the hearse and headed to Sarge's house. Ramona was waiting for us on the front porch. She gave us both a big hug. We headed down the little hall to the bedroom and lifted Sarge onto the stretcher. As we were leaving Ramona stopped us. "Danny, I want to play something for you on the stereo as you are leaving." I said, "Sure, whatever you want to do." Next thing we knew she was playing the "Battle Hymn of the Republic." *Mine eyes have seen the glory of the coming of the Lord...* I looked over at Steve and he was crying. Then I started crying. We cried all the way back to the funeral home.

We had his military funeral, with the honor guard, pallbearers from the army, 21-gun salute...and all; it was a very impressive service. I believe that Sarge had a premonition about his death, and thus needed to make amends with me. In my opinion, God grabbed hold of Sarge's heart. Thus, his hate for me turned into love. And my fear of him melted into total respect and admiration.

I'm glad Tolbert Stroud came into my life. *Rest in peace, Sarge.*

Posing with my two sisters Terry (middle) and
Cindy, 1963.

I got my fist hearing aid when I was in the fourth grade. It was called a "box" hearing aid and I hated it. Before long I was taking it off during my walk to school.

The Jefferson family, 1971

My first grade picture (1962, Hillcrest Elementary School) and my graduation picture with National Honor Society chords (1974, Walter Williams High School.)

Danny Jefferson

GUPTON JONES COLLEGE
Atlanta, Georgia

NAME Jefferson, Danny Lee
Burlington, North Carolina

SUBJECT	I QUARTER		II QUARTER		III QUARTER		IV QUARTER		Comp. Exam	Final Avg.	Qt. Hrs.	Gr. Pt.
	Grade	QT. Hrs.	Grade	QT. Hrs.	Grade	QT. Hrs.	Grade	QT. Hrs.				
Accounting			B	3								
Anatomy	B	3	A	3	A	2	A	2				
Chemistry & Toxicology	A	3	A	2	C	2	B	2				
Embalming	C	2	B	2	A	2	A	3				
First Aid												
Microbiology	A	3	B	2	B	3	A	2				
Mortuary Administration Funeral Directing	A	3	A	2	A	3	B	2				
Mortuary Business Law			A	2								
Pathology	A	3	A	3								
Psychology & Public Relations							B	3				
Public Health, Hygiene Sanitary Science												
Restorative Art.	A	2	A	1	A	4	A	2				
Business English	A	1										
Business Law					C	2						
R. A. Lab							A	1				
TOTALS												
General Average	92.839											

Remarks:

Graduated August 20, 1976

EXPLANATION OF GRADES: A candidate for graduation must have grade points equivalent to or exceeding the total number of quarter hours taken. Grade points are earned on the following schedule: A, 3; B, 2, C, 1; D, 0; F, 0; U, 0.

OFFICIAL
SEAL

SIGNATURE OF SCHOOL OFFICIAL

TITLE

My report card from Gupton-Jones
School of Mortuary Science, 1976

I started doing stand-up comedy routines in the early
1980s. This is the publicity shot that is used to promote
my appearances.

Making 'em laugh on the Carnival Cruise Line, in the
mid 1980s

I did a lot of modeling in the 1980s and 90s. This photo was featured in a national ad for a suit manufacturer

In 1983 I posed with Hanes Lineberry's futuristic
family limousine, which was actually a customized
RV. There was a place for the casket (the square door
behind me in the photo) and a place in the back for the
flowers. It accommodated twelve people and even had
a bathroom. This vehicle, called "The Blue Goose,"
turned out to be a bad (and very expensive) idea.

HOME FEDERAL

444 NORTH ELM STREET/PO BOX 26400/GREENSBORO NC 27420/(919) 373-5000

JIM MELVIN
Chairman of the Board

June 29, 1988

Mr. Danny Jefferson
General Chairman
Hospice Golf Tournament
Post Office Box 630
Greensboro, North Carolina 27402

Dear Danny:

I congratulate you for your splendid work in
putting on the Golf Tournament last week.
Everything was perfect. You deserve a great
deal of credit for this success. It is nice of
you to lend your talents to such a worthy
cause. You are certainly an outstanding young
fellow and I predict great things for you.

My best wishes for your continued success, and
thanks again for a job well done.

Sincerely,

Jim Melvin

sm

cc: Mr. A. S. Lineberry, Jr.

This letter was from Greensboro Mayor Jim
Melvin in 1988, the year I Chaired the Greensboro Hospice Golf Tournament.

This was my golf team in the 1988 Greensboro Hospice Golf Tournament. It included Wake Forest men's basketball coach, Bob Staak (far left) and TV sportscaster Johnny Phelps, (far right.) That's me in the middle.

lite

Meister Bräu

LÖWENBRÄU

Genuine Draft

I. H. CAFFEY DISTRIBUTING CO., INC.

July 1, 1988

Mr. Danny Jefferson
Hanes-Lineberry
515 North Elm Street
Greensboro, North Carolina

Dear Danny:

I would like to thank you for the tremendous amount of work
you put into the Hospice promotion. It seemed like every
time I turned around you were making things run just a little
more smoothly.

I have sponsored many special events over the years but I
have never worked with a more organized, dedicated group of
people. I feel the tournament was a tremendous success and
we certainly look forward to working with you again next
year. Thank you again.

Sincerely yours,

I. H. Caffey
President

IHC: kkb

Another thank you letter regarding the Hospice
promotion. This one was from I. H. Caffey, president of I. H. Caffey Distributing Company.

8749 U. S. Hwy. 421. W., Greensboro, NC 27409-9699   (919) 668-0876

Danny Jefferson

The Mayor's Committee for Persons with Disabilities
In Reidsville/Rockingham County

The Mayor's Committee is a Liaison arm of the North Carolina Department of Administration,
Governor's Advocacy Council for Persons with Disabilities

CLARK TURNER, MAYOR
230 West Morehead Street
Reidsville, North Carolina 27320
Telephone: 349-7013

CLINGMAN C. CAPPS, CHAIRMAN
2101 Richardson Drive
Reidsville, North Carolina 27320
Telephone: 349-2617

ELAINE YOST, VICE CHAIRPERSON
NELLIE CHISM, TREASURER
Katy Davis SECRETARY

October 22, 1987

Mr. Danny Lee Jefferson
Hanes-Lineberry Funeral Service
P.O. Box 630
Greensboro, N.C. 27402

Dear Danny:

I just wanted to write and thank you on behalf of the Mayor's
Committee for speaking at our banquet. You were absolutely
the highlight of the evening. Your talk was funny, entertaining,
and inspiring to all present. And it sure was nice to see that
handsome face.

I talked to Charlie Vitou on Wednesday and told him what you had
said and he said it absolutely made his day, that he remembered you
well, and promised me he would come by and see you. I wish we had
been able to let Charlie know in time for him to be present. ·

Again, thank you for really dressing up our banquet. (You're lucky
we let you leave).

Sincerely,

Katy Davis, Secretary

P.O. Box 67
Wentworth, N.C. 27375

Over the years I've spoken to many disability groups
and organizations. These people inspire me. My hearing loss is nothing compared to what many of these
people have had to endure.

In 1999 I was U.S. District 31-D Governor of Lions
Club International. The convention that year was
held in San Diego, California. Here I'm receiving
my medal from my counterpart, the Lions Club
District Governor of Japan, our sister club.

The Jefferson House, family visitation and hospitality house, is next door to Pierce-Jefferson Funeral Home. The atmosphere here feels more like home, and recaptures the tradition of how families of the deceased gathered in past times. It is a unique alternative to the traditional funeral home. The Jefferson House is one of just a few such facilities in the United States.

Pierce-Jefferson Funeral Home and Crematorium

IF AT FIRST YOU DON'T SUCCEED…

I believe it was in the early 80s when people started telling me how funny I was. I would tell jokes and funny stories and have my buddies doubling over in laughter. I was in my late twenties and working for Hanes Lineberry Funeral Home.

Funeral directors used to be called "undertakers" and most had a macabre sense of humor. It was corny stuff like, "People are dying to get in here," or, "Business is dead right now," or "Our funeral home has a lot of stiff competition." But that's not the kind of stuff I did. My humor was comprised more of jokes and storytelling. People have asked me if I was the class clown in school, but I absolutely was not. Since I couldn't hear, I pretty much kept to myself. I sure wasn't telling jokes and making people laugh. Because of my handicap, people laughed at me, not with me.

I'm not sure that a sense of humor is something anyone is born with. I think it's just how we look at life. And who may have influenced us along the way. We can choose to laugh or we can choose to cry. Laughter, I believe, is the best medicine. I always liked slapstick humor. How can you watch Abbott and Costello and not laugh, or the Three Stooges? Some people can maintain a sense of humor all the way to their deathbed. Oscar Wilde took this to the extreme when he uttered his last words, "Either me or this wallpaper has to go."

I don't know if I was born with a good sense of humor or not. But I know for sure that I was influenced by two of my uncles, Ronnie and Kenneth Webb, my mother's brothers. Uncle Ronnie and Uncle "Kenny Boy" would sit around and tell jokes and stories for hours. Although I couldn't hear what they were saying, I could read their lips like a book. And I remember everything until this day, word for word.

When God takes something away (hearing in my case) he gives something back in return. He gave me a photographic memory. But although I remember their jokes, I can't repeat most of them in mixed company. But they were real comedians and I loved listening to them. I could particularly relate to Kenny because he, too, was practically deaf. Never got hearing aids, though. By his own admission, he was just too vain.

In 1985 a comedy club opened in Greensboro called Twofers. It was located in the Forum 6 shopping and office building next to Friendly Shopping Center. I had heard good things about it and headed there one cold, wintry night in February to check it out. I laughed until my side hurt. The headliner that night was Lance Montalto. Comedy clubs typically have three acts. The first guy, known as the emcee, lays down the rules regarding behavior, etc. He also has an "act" that lasts three or four minutes tops. Then he introduces the next guy known as the "feature" act. His gig is about ten to fifteen minutes long. Then it was time for headliner Montalto. Typically, headline acts go for thirty to forty-five minutes. Montalto's opening routine went something like this:

"What happens if you're put in prison and your cell is next to a guy's who got life plus ten years? Well, you're okay until his life sentence is up. Then you're in big trouble. In two or three days you ask, "What is that smell?" And after about five days, "God, why are my eyes beginning to water." Then come the flies…thousands and thousands of green flies…"

Later on he did a routine about cereal. *"Who in the hell comes up with these names for cereals? Surely they have to be perverts. Who else could name a cereal Trix, or Fruit Loops? Or how about Grape Nuts and…Cocoa Puffs?"*

The next day I told some of my buddies what a great time I had. That's when the encouragement started. My good friend at Hanes Lineberry, Steve Blackwell, was the ringleader. "Danny," he said, "You're the funniest guy around. You need to try your hand at being a stand up comedian. They'll love you at Twofers!" How could I say no?

So I went a couple of weeks later and signed up, and was given a chance for my "fifteen minutes of fame." Actually, I was only allotted five minutes, tops. They have lights in comedy clubs to keep you on your toes. When the yellow light comes on you need to hurry up and end your routine. If the red light comes on you better end it fast, or they'll pull the plug on you, which is very embarrassing. Well, it was my time to perform. I forgot who the emcee was that night, but he stepped up to the microphone and said, "Put your hands together for Danny Jefferson." And here I came. The rest was a blur.

I bombed. I was horrible. I was supposed to be funny, and I was not funny at all. The jokes my buddies laughed at just didn't translate to that audience. Nobody laughed. I felt naked, and totally humiliated. It didn't make me sad, though. It made me mad. And fiercely determined to get it right the next time. So I started studying successful comedians, their body language, their delivery…and their timing. I learned that when you say something really funny, and people start laughing, you need to pause…and laugh with them. I studied the great ones like Bob Hope, Jack Benny and Johnny Carson. And Chris Rock, Rodney Dangerfield, George Carlin and Robin Williams. And I've probably patterned myself after the late, great Lewis Grizzard more than anyone else. I also learned that when you're doing comedy, you should make eye contact all over the place, with everyone in the room. After all, they're all paying money to see you!

After about six weeks, I felt like I had my act together and would give it another try. It was April of 1985. I showed up around seven-thirty at Twofers and met with Dana Lowell, who was booking the acts that night. Lowell is famous for playing Billy Bobb, who hosted Billy Bobb's Action Theatre on WGGT. He was named North Carolina's ShowTime'comedian of the year in 1986. Dana was a big time comedian who knew what he was doing. So when I asked to go first that night, he tried to talk me out of it. "Danny", he said, "you bombed when you first tried this. Now you want to go first? People aren't settled in yet. They haven't had enough to drink. This could be a disaster."

"Dana," I said. "I've got to do this. Then I'll know. If I screw up tonight my comedy days are over. But I've been practicing. I've been studying. I know I can pull this off."

"Ok Danny," said Dana. "But don't say I didn't warn you."

I learned by studying other comedians that just telling jokes doesn't work. You have to tell stories. And say things that completely catch the audience off guard. You have to make people laugh about every fifteen seconds. And that's exactly what I did that night when I was introduced at ten minutes after nine.

"If I say something that offends you tonight, please let me know…so I can say it again."

There was laughter all over the place. The ice was broken. I was on my way.

"Have you ever wondered why you drive on a parkway and park in a driveway?"

"My wife and I are flying again next week. And I will ask, again, why is there a flotation device under my seat instead of a parachute?"

"Ever been to Oklahoma and seen THE TREE? That place is so flat your dog can leave for three days and you can still see his tail. Put a Ford Fairmont in Oklahoma City and thousands will come out just to admire it."

"Ever wonder why they call it the Heartland? Because the brain isn't there!"

"And how about Iowa? Know what Iowa stands for? Idiots Out Walking Around. Had a big flood out there a few years ago and CNN showed two guys on top of a house. A baseball cap floats downstream below. Then floats back upstream 'What in the hell is that all about?' Asks one of the guys. To which the other guy replied, 'Well, grandpa did say he was going to mow the yard, come hell or high water?'"

"Hear about the guy who drowned last week after falling into a beer vat at the brewery in Eden. The insurance company, though, is refusing to pay.

Seems that hidden cameras show him getting out and going to the bathroom several times."

"Before I could afford a hearing aid, I stuck a button in my ear with a string tied to it. Didn't make me hear any better, but people sure talked a lot louder."

"Read a label the other night on a sleeping pill bottle that said, WARNING: THIS PRODUCT MAY MAKE YOU DROWSY."

"Ever noticed people with a car like yours waving like they're your friend?"

"Overshot the runway last week in Miami and landed in Cuba."

"Did you know there are no swimming pools in Cuba? If you can swim you swim to Miami."

"The new Barbie Doll just came out. It's called Divorced Barbie. It comes with all of Ken's stuff!"

"Mercedes Benz SUVs are now made in Alabama of all places. I sure hope they're easy to put together!"

Here are some actual announcements found in church bulletins:

"Don't let worry kill you. Let the church help."

"If you have children and don't know it, there is a nursery downstairs."

"There is a pinto bean supper every Wednesday night. Music will follow."

I finished my show that night to rousing applause. Later found out that I had actually won the competition. Within a period of six weeks, I went from being practically booed off the stage to winning the competition. In other words, I had gone from worst to first! I was a hit. Dana asked to me to come back as the emcee. Then I went on to perform at other clubs including Coconuts in Winston-Salem and the Cabana in the old Howard Johnson's in Greensboro. I even did a show once in Salisbury with Lance Montalto himself.

Most of these gigs were very tiring. I

was paid in cash and had to wait until all the money was accounted for, which was around midnight. I usually made around sixty dollars a night, which wasn't bad money back then. Sure beat working the second shift back at Annedeen Hosiery!

Things were going well for me. I had a good job. And was becoming well known as not only a stand up comedian, but a motivational speaker as well. Life was good. But something was missing. I was lonely. I longed for another relationship...someone to share my life with...

"OURS IS NOT TO REASON WHY…"

I met Kathy at a club in Greensboro in 1984 and we were married a year later. Marriage and the funeral business wasn't a good fit back in those days. Or maybe it just takes a while for people to mature. At least it did for me. But we live and learn. And we grow, too. I have no regrets, though. I believe everything happens for a reason. We live and learn. My first marriage didn't work out but God blessed Donna and me with our son, Jonathan. So I don't call that marriage a mistake. God had a plan for Donna and me too… and He still does.

I don't believe there are mistakes in God's universe. Everything happens according to His plan.

Over the years I have embalmed many babies. It's the toughest thing I ever have to do. And I've often asked how can bad people live to be a hundred while babies have to die. But I realize that I'm not actually embalming little babies. I'm just embalming their bodies. These babies are now little angels in Heaven. I take great solice in knowing that embalming is just a science. I deal with bodies. Not spirits...not souls.

The embalming room is the end of the road only for our earthly bodies. We will be made whole again. Although our marriage didn't last, I am sure that God put Kathy and me together. Why? Because He had a plan. Kathy had a lovely daughter, Nikki, by a former marriage. The saddest day of my life was when I lost Jonathan to adoption. One of the happiest days of my life came many years later...in 1992. That's when I legally adopted Nikki.

I love her as if she were my own. And I thank God for her.

DAY OF THE LIVING DEAD

In the early 1980s, Hanes Lineberry sent me to a Life Appreciation Seminar in West Virginia. There were about ten of us from different parts of the country, and we got to know each other very well. We learned what was important in life, and what wasn't.

The facilitator, Bill Bates, talked about a boiling tea pot…stuff keeps going in and it gets hotter and hotter, creating pressure which will eventually make it explode. We're like teapots. Daily pressures build up and unless we deal with them, we will sooner or later explode. It's like being stopped at a stoplight and looking for something in your glove compartment. The light turns green and the guy behind you starts honking his horn and shooting you the bird. Then you get all bent out of shape and speed off. Then you get to the office and throw your briefcase down, chew somebody out for no reason, and storm into your office. You stay in a bad mood all day and take it out on your wife when you get home that night. You let a horn - blowing jerk ruin a day that could have been happy and productive. Why?

The guy didn't hit you, he didn't steal from you...he didn't harm you in any way. But you let him get to you. Actually, though, you did it to yourself. In cases like this, think of the old adage, "Sticks and stones may break my bones but words will never hurt me."

No matter what this guy was saying back there (probably something disrespectful to your mother), they were just words. We have no control over other peoples' actions and behavior, but we have complete control on how we react to it. What we did on that day, and the questions they asked (such as what is your favorite color, and who is the first girl you ever kissed), still stick out in my mind. By the way, my favorite color is blue, and the first girl I ever kissed was Paula Sue Byrd.

When I was in the first grade at Hillcrest Elementary in Burlington, I jumped up from beside the water cooler and planted one right on her cheek. Of course if you did that today you would be expelled.

I told that story at one my high school reunions and a Greek girl, Jackie Touloupas (Harrell) came up and said, "I'm very disappointed. I thought I was the first girl you ever kissed." "Lord," I replied. "I don't even remember kissing *you!*"

They also had questions like," What do you enjoy doing most." In spite of my bad knee (which required reconstructive surgery in 2013), the first things that came to mind were golf and tennis. Other questions included who do you enjoy being around the most. Of course I mentioned my immediate family, but I also listed my mother's brother, the aforementioned "Uncle Kenny Boy."

They told me that I could make one phone call before the sequestered three-day session was to begin. I called my ex-wife, Donna, and pretty much apologized for the fact that things didn't work out between us…and that I had no choice but to leave her and Jonathan. It scared her. She even called my boss at Hanes Lineberry and said she was afraid I was going to commit suicide.

They also asked me who my favorite teacher was, and how she would eulogize me. I wasn't sure about the eulogy part, but my favorite teacher was Mrs. Garner, my 10th grade history teacher at Burlington Williams. Her daughter, Virginia, was actually in the same class. Mrs. Garner was always frustrated with me because I would never pay attention. I didn't pay attention because I couldn't hear. But I loved history and made good grades. I could see the chalkboard and I could read and study the books. And basically that was what I was doing; reading the books while Mrs. Garner was talking.

When you're deaf, you figure out ways to function, even ways to wake up when you're sound asleep. Years ago they came out with a device that would blink the lights and shake the bed when the phone rang. They didn't have one at Hanes Lineberry (for those night shift duties) so I placed a metal sign on my stomach and put the phone on top. That way the phone would vibrate the sign and wake me up. Ironically, the sign said, "Slow. Funeral."

When we were in the second day of the seminar we learned why we were asked so many questions. The questions were the basis of our "eulogies." One by one, we would lay on the floor, covered by a white sheet, while one of us read a eulogy. After about the third eulogy, it was my turn to get under the sheet.

"Danny Jefferson overcame a severe handicap to achieve great things in life," my eulogizer said. "He was not pretentious in any way. He was a down-to-earth guy whose favorite food was Zack's Hot Dogs. His favorite teacher was Mrs. Garner, one of his tenth grade teachers at Burlington Williams. She was always frustrated with him, though, because he didn't appear to ever pay attention. But he made good grades...even made the National Honor Society. And he was a great comedian. People loved to be around Danny. He always made them laugh and feel good." By this time I was trembling and crying…

"He gave his Uncle Kenny Boy a lot of credit for his sense of humor," my eulogizer said. "God replaced Danny's deafness with a photographic memory. He even remembered the first girl he ever kissed, Paula Sue Byrd, when he was in the first grade. Danny was a kind and good man who gave back to the community, over and over. He will be missed by everyone who had the good fortune of knowing him…"

It went on and on. My "funeral" was the most intense thing I had ever gone through in my life. And I felt great relief getting out from under that sheet! "Life Appreciation" was certainly an appropriate name for this seminar…

"BITTER BLOOD"

In June of 1985, when I was at Hanes Lineberry, we were notified by the Greensboro Police Department that we needed to pick up the bodies of two young boys, John and Jim Lynch. They were the children of Susie Newsom of Winston-Salem, North Carolina and her ex-husband Tom Lynch, a New Mexico dentist. The two were in a fierce custody battle for the boys. She also was seriously involved with her first cousin, Fritz Klenner of Reidsville. Klenner, who claimed he had gone to Duke, was practicing medicine without a license.

Klenner was a habitual liar who also claimed to be an agent with the CIA. He was an extreme right wing survivalist and an avid supporter of the Ku Klux Klan. And he was a dedicated admirer of Adolph Hitler.

In the summer of 1984, family members of Tom Lynch and Susie Newsom were murdered in cold blood. Lynch's mother and sister were killed on July 22, 1984 as they returned from church in Oldham County, Kentucky. Then, on May 18, 1985, Susie's father, Bob Newsom, her mother Florence, and grandmother Hattie were shot to death in their home in Winston-Salem. Before he was killed, Bob Newsom was to have testified in the child custody case in favor of Lynch.

By June 1985 Greensboro police and SBI agents had substantial evidence and were closing in on Newsom and Klenner. But on June 3rd, as they approached the Greensboro apartment complex where the couple lived, Klenner opened fire. Then the couple and boys fled in an SUV. After about a fifteen-minute chase the SUV was stopped near Guilford College. Klenner promptly opened fire with a machine gun; wounding three officers. Then he detonated an explosive charge, blowing up himself and his three passengers.

I was given the gruesome task of embalming the bodies of those two little boys. We don't know what they did with Klenner's body. We assumed they sent what was left of it to a funeral home in Reidsville. Susie was probably sitting directly over the bomb, because the lower half of her body was completely decimated.

I discovered in the embalming room that the boys didn't actually die from the explosion. They were already dead from cyanide poisoning...BEFORE *they were both shot in the head!*

We took their caskets to what was then called the Greensboro/Winston-Salem/High Point Airport for their flight home to Albuquerque, New Mexico. Tom Lynch was there...waiting for his sons.

Three years later, in 1988, *Bitter Blood: A true story of southern family pride, madness and multiple murder*, written by Jerry Bledsoe, reached No. 1 on the New York Times bestseller list. A movie by the same name debuted in 1994 on the Lifetime Movie Network.

JON

When my son Jonathan was fourteen, a friend of mine, Joe Gamble (actually one of Jon's teachers), got us tickets to a play that Jon was singing in at school. Of course I couldn't approach him. All I could do was sit in the audience and watch him sing. I hadn't seen him since he was a baby, but I had no trouble picking him out. When it was over, Jon recognized Joe and approached us. Joe said, "Great play Jon. Didn't know you were such a great singer. Oh…I'd like for you to meet my friend, Danny." Jon and I shook hands and exchanged pleasantries.

He had no idea who I was. Not the slightest.

Four years later, in 1997, Jon paged me (don't remember exactly how he got my number) on the night of his Senior Prom. "Dad," he said. "This is Jon. I'm trying to get in touch with you. Here's my number. I'm going to bed now, but would you please call me in the morning?" I called the next morning and his friend Chad answered the phone. "This is Danny," I said, " and I'm calling to speak to Jon." Knowing who I was, he replied, "Oh…Mr. Jefferson, this is Chad. Jon's still asleep. I'll have him call you as soon as he gets up." "Thanks, Chad. Tell him I can't wait to hear from him." When I hung up the phone I lost it. I went to the bathroom and cried like a baby. Glad I lived alone so no one could see me like that. When I pulled myself together I called my mother to tell her the news. While she and I were talking I heard the phone click. It was Jon calling me back.

We talked about an hour and a half. He said he couldn't see me for a couple of weeks because he was going to Washington, D.C. with his choral group. When he returned, he left a message and invited me to a softball game he was playing in. The game was in late April, a couple weeks after his eighteenth birthday.

I got there that morning, sat in the stands, and watched him play. After the game, he introduced me to his coach and all of his teammates. He had told everyone that I was coming. He and I then headed to Biscuitville where we spent about an hour and half. We talked about everything we could think of, including his late May high school graduation. Couldn't wait, since he knew I could show up, legally. We talked about a big Mother's Day get-together at my mother's house in Burlington and how it would be a "coming out party" for him.

I picked Jon up at Chad's that morning and we were on our way. And what a day it was. Jon was not only the son I never got to know. He was my mother's first grandchild she never got to know. I was so proud of Jon that day. He had the foresight to bring pictures of himself to hand out to every family member there. It was like he had been an active part of the Jefferson family all of his life! It was a great day.

The next big event was the graduation,

which I knew would be a bittersweet experience. Frankly, I dreaded seeing my ex-wife and her husband. But my son is now eighteen and no one can stop me from seeing him. I will be there with bells on. So I called his mother and told her as much. "I will keep my distance," I told her. "Don't worry about me nosing into the family pictures or anything like that. But my eighteen years of purgatory are up. And from now on, I will have a relationship with my son. And no one can stop me."

I kept my word. I went to the graduation and stayed out of everybody's way. I got nowhere near Jon's mother and her husband. But I know I was the proudest parent there. I choked up when Jon was handed his diploma. Just wish they had called him by a different name. But changing his name would have to be his decision. I'm sure, though, that the only thing on Jon's mind was his and Chad's celebration trip to Myrtle Beach.

A few days into the beach trip Jon left me a voicemail message: "Dad, I've been thinking about something. How do you feel about the name Jon *Jefferson?*"

TURNING DISABILITIES INTO ABILITIES

I firmly believe that when God takes something away from you, he gives you something in return; something that will more than compensate for a handicap, which in my case was being born legally deaf.

There are people who don't have arms who are using their feet to write. I know a gentleman who lives in Chapel Hill who doesn't have any arms. He wears sandals and eats with his feet. He opens the doors with his feet. I don't pretend to know what his life has been like. I just can't imagine. Compared to him, I don't have any problems. I spoke to the Orange County Disability Association a few years ago and he was there. After the speech, he joined us for dinner... eating with his feet, and not at all self-conscious. He had a wonderful attitude. You didn't hear him whining about anything. His positive attitude was an inspiration to me. I'm sure when he's out in public that people gape at him and think he's a freak. But that's their problem, not his.

People used to make fun of me, too. I talked too much and I talked too loud. That's what people do who can't hear. God, though, gave me abilities that made up for my handicap. For one, He gave me a photographic memory. When I'm talking to families about their arrangements, I don't write anything down. I don't have to. I remember everything, right down to their social security numbers. And when I ditched my vanity and started wearing two hearing aids, God gave me the ability to become a good listener. And when you listen, you become more compassionate. And when you become more compassionate, you become more empathetic. Compassion and empathy are characteristics that a successful funeral director must possess.

Every family who walks into a funeral home is different, but they are there for the same reason. They've lost a loved one. A loved one who has the same blood, the same hair, the same eyes...the same skin; everything except what made them eat, sleep, talk and think...Every grieving family must be treated with dignity and respect, regardless of their status in life.

Over the years, at Lowe, Sechrest, Hanes Lineberry and Pierce-Jefferson, I've been involved in thousands of funerals; each one unique in itself. Some are more emotional than others. I've comforted, hugged and held the hands of thousands of people. But I haven't cried (at least not in public), although I've wanted to - especially when babies or young children are buried. I've also been inspired by surviving children, one in particular was a little nine-year-old boy.

Several years ago he was playing inside with his brother, who was eleven. The nine-year-old ran out the back door as his brother followed. The storm door slammed and the older boy ran up and tried to push it open, shattering the glass. He fell forward onto an arrow shaped shard, puncturing his lung. The boy was dead within minutes.

During the visitation at the funeral home, the little nine-year-old was sitting alone as the adults mingled. So I took him to an office to console him. When he walked in he headed straight to a typewriter. I said, "Why don't you type the names of your family? He started pecking away. He typed his dad's name, his mom's name, his dead brother's name…and then his own name. I rolled out the paper and said, "So…there's your family…you've typed the names of your whole family." He paused for a second, put his forefinger over his brother's name, and said, "No…that's my family now." "You're right, son," I said. "You're right."

I put my arm around him and led him back to the parlor. He seemed to be doing fine. But I was choking back tears.

GRANDMA & CHARLIE

When I was little I spent a lot of time with my grandmother in Roxboro. She was my mother's mother and she was old school all the way. She even had an old school name, Flossie. Her house was tiny. Instead of two rooms and a bath it was "one room and a path." An old coal stove in what she called the living room provided the heat. You couldn't get near the thing; much less touch it. It was like living in a steam room without the steam. I've been hot natured to this day and I believe it's because of my days burning up at Grandma

Webb's house.

Her cooking was old school, too. She had a chicken coop in her backyard, which provided cheap (and bloody) entertainment for me. Grandma would go to the coop, grab a chicken by its feet and head to the old tree stump. There she would hold it down, grab her hatchet, and chop its head off. The term, "Running around like a chicken with its head cut off," was a literal event in granny's little back yard. Then she put it in boiling water, plucked its feathers out, cleaned it and chopped it up into breasts, thighs, legs and wings. Then she soaked the pieces in buttermilk before rolling them in flour. Next she carefully placed each piece, one at a time, in a large iron skillet, just as the Crisco gently began to bubble. Talk about good eating! Colonel Sanders chicken couldn't hold a candle to it.

Grandma was set in her ways and you couldn't change her thinking. For instance, she never believed that men walked on the moon. She thought the whole thing was faked. Not so with wrestling. She dearly loved watching wrestling on TV and believed that every bit of it was 100 percent real. It was the era when big name wrestlers like George Becker, Swede Hansen and Johnny Weaver were in their heyday. Granny would stand in front of the little black and white TV and scream, holler and wave her arms.

Back then the wrestling announcer was Charlie Harville, the legendary sports director at WFMY TV, Channel 2, in Greensboro. The first wrestling matches televised, and announced by Harville, took place in the Lexington, N.C. YMCA on May 1, 1954. In 1958, the Lexington "Y" hosted the first ever World Heavyweight Wrestling Championship, also announced by Harville. Charlie loved all sports but couldn't quite cut it as an athlete. So he pursued his second ambition, being a sports broadcaster.

While still at High Point College, he landed a job down the road at WMFR Radio, announcing Thomasville High School football and baseball games. World War II came along soon, though, and Charlie was drafted. After an honorable discharge from the Army Air Corps, he was back in radio at several stations including WLPO in LaSalle, Illinois. It was there that he coined the unique closing phrase he would use until the end of his career, "That's The Best In Sports Today."

Charlie died when he was eighty-three and his daughter, Linda, worked with me at Hanes Lineberry on the arrangements. On March 6 we arranged the visitation for family and friends at Bryan Park Enrichment Center. Charlie had eleven children and a countless number of friends and fans. Hundreds of people from all walks of life showed up. Then we had the funeral, for the immediate family, at home plate in War Memorial Stadium in Greensboro, America's oldest minor league stadium. Charlie had donated his body to science… and it was later cremated. And since he was a veteran, we placed the American flag in his usual seat on the first base line. It was stirring…and very emotional.

It was Charlie's wish that his ashes be scattered over his favorite golf course, Monroeton, a short, country track between Greensboro and Reidsville. With Charlie's connections, he could have played anywhere. Sedgefield, Starmount… the Greensboro Country Club…anywhere! But he loved this little golf course in the middle of nowhere.

So a friend of mine, Chuck Armentrout, and I headed out there and played eighteen holes. And we scattered a little bit of Charlie on every hole.

We hit our balls and scattered Charlie... hit our balls and scattered Charlie. When we putted out on number eighteen, I put Charlie's remaining ashes in the cup. Then I replaced the flagstick, looked at my buddy, and said, "That's The Best In Sports Today!"

DISRESPECTING THE DEAD: A TRAVESTY

Todd Van Beck, a noted Abraham Lincoln scholar, is a good friend of mine. I've always been a history buff and am fascinated with his knowledge. He even dresses the part. Every day, like Lincoln, he wears a black suit and white shirt. He is very knowledgeable in other areas, too. And he's always taken a keen interest in what I do for a living.

He recently made an observation about the funeral business that's been bothering me for a long time: Hospitals and nursing homes will do anything to hide the fact that people actually die there.

There is a nursing home in the eastern part of North Carolina that won't let hearses on the premises. The body must be picked up by an unmarked van. That seems to be the trend. Little white, unmarked vans are being requested by hospitals and nursing homes to pick up bodies. Simply, especially at hospitals, hearses are taboo. I don't know why. You'll never see a hearse in front of a hospital anyway.

I tell my guys when they go to an unfamiliar hospital to pick up a body just to look for the dumpsters. Hospital administrators want the bodies to come out through the bowels of the hospital. The morgues are always near the kitchens where refrigeration and plumbing are convenient.

The entrance and exit doors used by funeral directors to carry out bodies are the same doors used by kitchen staffers to take out the garbage. It's a disgrace.

I once heard a quote that said, "Show me in the manner in which a country treats its dead and I will show you within mathematically equivalent, how successful that country is."

The dead should be treated with dignity and respect.

WHAT A JOURNEY

In 1988 Loewen, later to be called the Alderwoods Group, a giant funeral home and cemetery conglomerate acquired Hanes Lineberry. They made me sales manager of twenty-six cemeteries and eleven funeral homes from Wallace to Mars Hill, North Carolina. I was making in the low six figures, the most money I had ever made in my life. In 1997 Loewen even asked me to do a stand up comedy routine at its annual convention in Las Vegas.

The convention was held at the MGM Grand. With over 5,000 rooms, it was the largest hotel in the world at the time. The lobby was themed after MGM's 1939 legendary film, *The Wizard of Oz.* To enter the MGM, you walked beneath a giant cartoon-like version of Leo the Lion, but this was later changed. Seems that Chinese high rollers, due to their feng shui beliefs, feared that entering the mouth of a lion was bad luck.

The showroom where I performed was huge, too. It probably accommodated at least three thousand people. I was used to intimate comedy clubs. But here, people were looking at the big screen videos instead of me. But I did okay. As a matter of fact, the producer booked me for a gig at a small comedy club within the MGM for the next two nights.

"Hello, I'm Danny Jefferson. And I'm so glad that I can be here tonight...because people like you make me feel halfway normal!"

Things were going well for me. I had a good job. And was becoming well known as not only a stand up comedian, but a motivational speaker as well. But there is a thin line between comedy and tragedy. The bad news struck on December 2, 2002 when I was laid off. Business had gotten a little tight and they got rid of me because of my big salary. I had to sign a non-compete agreement, which meant I could not get a job working in the funeral profession. I got a job selling supplemental insurance and I hated it. And I made very little money.

Things got worse. In August of 2003 I tore my hamstring while trying to water ski. I was laid up for three months. I had no money. No job. No health insurance. No "nothing." I was behind on everything. I had gone from making six figures in 2002 to an all-time low in 2004 of $3,900. About all I had was electricity and water. My cable TV had been cut off due to non-payment. So I read everything I could get my hands on. It was good for me. Not being able to watch TV was actually a blessing.

As I've said many times before, when God takes something away, he replaces it with something else. But I was destitute. In June of that year I got a foreclosure notice. I was about to lose my townhouse. I hated to do it, but I went to my dad to borrow enough money to keep it. He came through, and loaned me $4,000. I got to keep my townhouse. But I was flat broke.

So on September 14, 2004, I took all of my loose change to Food Lion across town where nobody would know me. I dumped it all into the Coin Star machine and left with a grand total of $142.38. And the worse was yet to come. I filed for bankruptcy later that month. Jon and I had to turn in our two Ford Explorers to the bank as part of the agreement. Jon never knew why we had to turn in the vehicles. Thankfully, I was able to keep the townhouse. Then opportunity knocked.

Funeral home conglomerate Service Corporation International contacted me. They wanted to talk with me about running ten of their funeral homes in the Corpus Christi, Texas area. They sent me plane tickets for the red eye to Houston, Texas and then a puddle jumper to Corpus Christi. The interviews went well. In late October they offered me the job. The salary was low six figures. And they were going give me $5,000 for moving expenses as well as buying my townhouse. They wanted an answer by November 5. By that time I was talking with Jack Pierce and Bill

Gaffney, president of the Citadel Group, about purchasing Pierce Funeral Home. Bill Gaffney gave me his word that it was doable. So I turned down the job in Texas. We shook hands on it. And that was it.

In the meantime, Jack and I formed a partnership and I actually was getting a salary for the first time in two years. Now, here I was, bankrupt, and wanting to buy a funeral home. Jack and I were able to negotiate with Citadel and took ownership - with Jack's money - in December 2004. My dear friend Jack died on October 30, 2005. Our agreement allowed me the opportunity to purchase the business from the Pierce family.

In January 2005 I opened a checking account at Fidelity Bank in Kernersville. Brenda Holbrook was the lady I worked with there. I gave her my social security number and then the bankruptcy red flags went up. But Brenda turned out to be great. I told her I wanted to buy a business and needed to talk with someone. She set up an appointment for me with senior vice president, Bob Reed. He was very nice but couldn't make any promises. He later called in executives from the home office for consultation. With nothing but the run down funeral home as collateral, I got the loan on a six-year note.

I will be eternally grateful to Bob Reed and the late Jack Pierce. My employees and I went to see Bob on February 1, 2011 and made the final payment. I owned Pierce-Jefferson Funeral Home, free and clear. It was the second happiest day of my life. The happiest day was April 15, 2006… the day I married Rosette Ambrose!

DEDICATION

In late 2010 my sister Cindy began experiencing severe headaches. Nothing she did seemed to alleviate the pain. She was transported by ambulance to Duke University Medical Center in Durham on a Monday in early January 2011. Neurologists there, who performed the seven -hour brain surgery on Senator Edward Kennedy, are recognized as being among the best in the world. An MRI revealed a tumor in her brain that would require surgery. The tumor was successfully removed two days later. Cindy and my parents were told that they would be called as soon as possible with a pathology report – which would reveal whether the tumor was benign or malignant.

Exactly one week after the surgery I called Mom and told her I would be bringing lunch. So I headed to Zack's in Burlington and picked up a bag of their legendary hot dogs. When I got to Mom and Dad's house, where Cindy was staying to recover, I realized that my younger sister, Terry, was also there. So it was just the family…the five of us. Ironically, we got the call from Duke while we were eating. It was devastating news. Cindy had brain cancer: Glioblastoma, Grade IV. She was given a year to live. We all started crying and holding on to each other.

Cindy went downhill fast as the experimental treatments she agreed to took their toll.

Christmas of 2011 was sad beyond belief, because we knew it would be Cindy's last. She knew it too. By the second week in January 2012 she started losing her motor skills, and the use of her left arm and left leg. But she did have a final request: She loved Myrtle Beach and wanted to go there one more time. So Rosette, my sister Terry and I gladly took her down there. It was around the middle of February 2012 and cold as the dickens. She loved the Sea Captain's House and that's where we had lunch on Valentine's Day. When we finished eating I rolled her out to the sea wall where she could see the ocean for one last time. It was breezy, cold and cloudy. We hadn't seen the sun the whole trip.

But that was soon to change. Cindy could still use her right arm and started pointing it to the sky. "Look at that," she exclaimed. "There it is. The sun has finally come out! And look at the ocean and those colors... the blues...the greens -just beautiful." She was happy and laughing. It was like God had parted the sky and shined upon her face. The trip, though, would be her last... at least in a car.

Two weeks later she was in an ambulance, heading to the hospice home in Burlington. I visited her every day and every night. Three weeks went by and she kept hanging on. Hospice did a wonderful job. They provided great comfort and support to Cindy. If there are angels among us, and I believe there are, I count hospice doctors and nurses among them.

In late March, about four weeks into Cindy's stay, my mother called and said I should get down there in a hurry. In my business you see horrible stuff all the time: bodies maimed from head on collisions, bullet wounds…and bodies burned beyond recognition. And I've seen it all. But I couldn't bear the thought of watching my sister die. So I thought of every possible thing I could do, or errand I could run, to delay the trip. But it didn't work. Cindy was determined to hang on until I got there. And she did. I went in, walked over to her bed, and kissed her on the forehead. Then I held her in my arms. Her breathing became more labored. She was dead within minutes. Even when we know that death is imminent, we're never prepared for it. "I love you, Cindy," I said. "I love you."

We all wept. My mother came apart. She had always said that there was nothing worse than losing a child. And she had just lost her oldest one. I comforted my mother as best I could. I called Jon and he drove down in the hearse. I knew it was going to be very, very difficult. But I was going to have to embalm my own sister. No one but my son, Jon, and I would touch her. Simply, it was a job we had to do. We held ourselves together during the two- hour procedure of embalming and restoration. Though it was the body of my own sister, it was still just a body...skin and bones. This body was no more my sister than a photo of her would have been. What made my sister my sister was her spirit...her soul. And her spirit and soul were no longer on this earth.

We placed her body in a casket and took it to Burlington for visitation and viewing. The funeral was held at Deep Creek Baptist Church where Cindy played the piano and taught Sunday school. The church and cemetery where Cindy was buried are right beside my parents' house. My mother visits her grave every day. Although she was only eleven months and twenty-four days older than me, I considered her my "big" sister. And I will forever miss her...

At Christmastime we honor the deceased whose funeral arrangements were handled at Pierce-Jefferson that year. We invite the immediate families to this candlelight service in our chapel. Town officials - mayor, town manager and police chief - read the names of the deceased. In 2012 we honored 180 souls. It is a very emotional experience. The 2012 service was particularly emotional for my family and me, because one of the names on the list was Cindy's. I sat on the front row with my parents and Rosette.

After the service we give each surviving family an angel Christmas ornament adorned with the name of their loved one. Lots of tears...lots of hugs. The service is sad... but also uplifting, heartwarming and inspirational.

It ends with a soloist singing...

"I MISS YOU MOST AT CHRISTMASTIME"

I miss you in the springtime, when flowers adorn the veil,
I miss you in the summer when raindrops follow hail,
I miss you in the autumn when God's greens cross the earth
I miss you in the winter and all the cold days through
I miss you most at Christmastime when choirs of angels sing
Peace on earth, good will to men and crown the newborn King...

EPILOGUE

Raymond Reid

"MANY ARE CALLED,
BUT FEW ARE CHOSEN."
Matthew 22:14

Danny Jefferson never let his handicap keep him from striving to be the best at everything he's undertaken to do. Many years ago he promised God that he would always give back. There is no statute of limitations as to when Danny stops giving. Stewardship is a lifelong commitment for him: So far so good.

He has served as Chairman for the Körner's Folly Foundation and a Board member of Care Net Counseling Center, as well as the Natural Science Center of Greensboro. He is a member of the Kernersville Lions Club and is a past District Governor for Lions District 31-D. He has served on the Board for Hospice, the Music Academy of North Carolina, the Shepherd's Center, Kernersville Chamber of Commerce, the former Downtown Council and CrimeStoppers. He has chaired numerous fundraising committees and has helped raise over $3 million for various charities around the Triad of North Carolina. He is a 1977 graduate of the Dale Carnegie Institute, where he finished second in his class. He is also a graduate of Leadership Kernersville.

Danny is a widely sought after motivational speaker where he begins each session with his hilarious stand up comic stints. When it comes to grieving families, Danny and his staff offer the utmost in compassion and empathy. Everyone who walks into Pierce-Jefferson is treated the same. Several years ago Danny started providing a service at

Pierce-Jefferson that few people know about. Families of public servants such as police officers, firefighters and EMS personnel are not charged for the funeral service if the loved one was killed in the line of duty. There's never a charge for infants' funerals, either. The costs are covered by the funeral home's Angel Support Fund.

Danny has led the way in making Pierce-Jefferson one of the most unique funeral homes in the country. The main funeral home has evolved from Kernersville's oldest home into a masterpiece of 19th century grace and elegance.

Danny recently added Kernersville's only crematorium, perfectly blended architecturally, to the funeral home.

Next-door is the newly opened Jefferson House, where families can host friends and relatives of the deceased. It contains flatscreen TVs throughout the house so videos of the deceased can be viewed. It also contains a kitchen area so meals can be brought in and served. "The Reflections Room" has been moved from the funeral home to the Jefferson House. It resembles a home's bedroom where the deceased can be placed in repose allowing family members to pay their last respects in an intimate... "homey" setting.

Danny is the consummate community leader, businessman and counselor, as well as a devoted family man. He and Rosette have four children, Jonathan, Nikki, Joshua and Jordan.

Danny is also a loyal friend to many. I consider myself lucky to be one of them.

And I am honored to have played a small role in the telling of his remarkable story.

CPSIA information can be obtained
at www.ICGtesting.com
Printed in the USA
FFOW03n0525301015
18179FF